For:

_____

From:

_____

Date:

_____

My child, believe what I say.
And remember what I command you.
Listen to wisdom.
Try with all your heart to gain understanding.
Cry out for wisdom.
Beg for understanding.
Search for it as you would for silver.
Hunt for it like hidden treasure.
Then you will understand what it means to respect the Lord.
Then you will begin to know God.
Only the Lord gives wisdom.
Knowledge and understanding come from him.

—Proverbs 2:1–6

READ AND SHARE™
Our
Together-Time
Bible

Gwen Ellis

Illustrations by Steve Smallman
and Jeffrey Ebbeler

THOMAS NELSON
Since 1798

NASHVILLE   DALLAS   MEXICO CITY   RIO DE JANEIRO   BEIJING

Published in Nashville, Tennessee, by Thomas Nelson. Thomas Nelson is a registered trademark of Thomas Nelson, Inc.

Scripture quotations are taken from INTERNATIONAL CHILDREN'S BIBLE®. © 1986, 1988, 1999 by Thomas Nelson, Inc. Used by permission.

Stories retold by Gwen Ellis
Illustrations by Steve Smallman and Jeffrey Ebbeler
Page Design by Casey Hooper

Works by Gwen Ellis © 2008, used by permission.
Works by June Ford © 2008, used by permission.
Works by Laura Minchew © 2008, used by permission.

Thomas Nelson, Inc., titles may be purchased in bulk for educational, business, fund-raising, or sales promotional use. For information, please e-mail SpecialMarkets@ThomasNelson.com.

Library of Congress Cataloging-in-Publication Data

Ellis, Gwen.
  Our together-time Bible / by Gwen Ellis ; illustrations by Steve Smallman and Jeffrey Ebbeler.
      p. cm.
  Includes index.
  ISBN 978-1-4003-1279-5 (hardcover)
  1. Bible stories, English. I. Smallman, Steve. II. Ebbeler, Jeffrey. III. Title.
  BS551.3.E545 2008
  220.9'505--dc22

                                                                                                2008007027

Printed in China
10 11 12 MT 6 5 4 3 2
MFG: MULTI TARGET

SHATIN,HONG KONG
APRIL 2010/# 105833

For John Mark

Dear Parents

Spending quality together time with your family is easy and fun with this book of 52 Bible-inspired topics. You'll be creating memories while helping your children develop the life skills they need as they discover how events in the Bible really do relate to their lives today.

In each devotional I've included a variety of age-appropriate topic introductions (ranging from songs and poems to recipes and stories), a Bible verse (short enough for a child to memorize), a Bible story, "Let's Talk about It" questions, a "Share God's Love" activity, and a prayer. As a bonus, this book can be used alone or alongside the *Read and Share Bible* storybook.

My prayer is that you and your family will begin a tradition of together time that will bring joy into your lives long past the conclusion of this book.

Blessings,
Gwen Ellis

Tips on How to Use This Book

· Choose one topic a week to read and discuss with your children or class. The more you create fun and lively discussions, the more your children will respond, listen, and look forward to your next together time.

· Read the short stories, poems, songs, and Bible stories in an entertaining way. Then encourage your children to act out the scene using different voices for different characters.

· Involve older children as readers.

· Encourage children to talk about the topic during mealtime, drive time, etc., throughout the week.

· Have each child think of ways that the topic relates to his or her life and then encourage the child to apply it.

· Do the activity (which may include playing games, creating crafts, baking, or discussing the topic) sometime during the week.

Contents

God Made Them All

Through his power all things were made—things in heaven and on earth, things seen and unseen. —COLOSSIANS 1:16

Did you know God made everything? He made all the beautiful and wonderful things we see: birds, fish, elephants, puppies, kittens, flowers, you, and me—everything! God made it all. How wonderful and awesome God is! Together let's celebrate what He has made by saying or singing the poem below.

ALL THINGS
BRIGHT AND BEAUTIFUL

All things bright and beautiful,
All creatures great and small,
All things wise and wonderful,
The Lord God made them all.
—Cecil Alexander (excerpt)

1

Genesis 1–2

In the beginning God made heaven and earth. Then God said, "Let there be light. Let there be plants. Let there be living things in the oceans. Let there be birds in the sky. Let there be animals on earth." And every time God said, "Let there be . . ." it happened!

Then God made people. First He made Adam. Later He made Eve so Adam would not be alone. God made both Adam and Eve like Himself. And God said it was all "Good"!

Our Together Time

Let's Talk about It!
★ What are some other things God made?
★ Who did God make to be like Himself?
★ What did God say about everything He had made?

Share God's Love
A fun way to celebrate all the bright and beautiful things God made is to make a creation collage of pictures. Ask a grownup to help you with this activity. Find some magazines that everyone has finished reading, a large piece of paper, and a pencil, pen, or crayon. At the top of your paper write: God Made Them All. Next, tear out or cut out pictures of things God has made. Glue as many of these pictures as you can onto the paper. Hang your paper with all the pictures in your room and thank God every day for all the things He has made. When friends see the collage of pictures on your wall, share God's love by telling them how God created the world.

Prayer
Dear Lord, thank You for making our beautiful world and all the animals, birds, and fish. Thank You for making everyone I love and for making me too. Amen.

Patient Noah

We show that we are servants of God by living a pure life,
by our understanding, by our patience, and by our kindness.
—2 CORINTHIANS 6:6

A patient person waits calmly and without complaining. How patient
are you? Is it hard for you to wait your turn when playing a game or to
wait to eat just-baked cookies? What about waiting for your birthday
or to open Christmas gifts?

Here's a fun way to find out how patient you really are. (To
make it even more fun, include other family members.)
Set a timer for one minute. Then sit perfectly still,
not moving a muscle except to breathe. Did it
seem as if one minute would never pass? Set the
timer again, and this time while you are waiting
have someone tell a story. Did the time go faster
when you were busy? Staying busy and doing
something useful while being
patient is a good plan.

In today's Bible story,
see how patiently
Noah waited in the
big boat with all
those smelly
animals.

5

Genesis 7:12; 8:1–19

You may know the story of Noah and how God saved Noah and his family from a big flood. Noah obeyed God and built a big boat, sometimes called Noah's Ark, and filled it with animals just as God told him to do. But did you know that they were in the boat for more than a year? That is a long time to be in a floating zoo! Everyone and every creature on that ark practiced patience as they waited for the day to come when they could leave the boat.

One day Noah went to the top of the boat and opened the window he had made. He sent a dove out to see if it could find dry land. If it did, they could get off the boat. The bird came back because it couldn't find a dry place to land. Noah waited seven days and sent the dove out again. This time it came back with a green leaf in its mouth. He waited seven more days and sent the bird out again, and this time it did not come back. Noah knew that meant the dove had found a safe home, because the water on the ground was drying up. Soon Noah and his family could get off the boat. Their waiting would be over.

Our Together Time

Let's Talk about It!
* How long were Noah, his family, and the animals on the ark?
* What did everyone on that boat have to practice?
* How many times did Noah send the dove out to find land?

Share God's Love
Yikes! Just think what it would be like to not go outside for a whole year. Being patient isn't easy, but it is something God wants us to do. There are lots of different ways to keep busy while you're being patient.

✤ On a car trip try acting out different animals sleeping or seeing how many cars you can count in your favorite color.
✤ At home you might read a book or play a game.

What are other things you can do while you're being patient?

Prayer
Dear Lord, please help me to be patient in everything I do. And thank You for being patient with me. Amen.

Being Cheerful and Kind

Do not forget to do good to others. And share with them what you have. These are the sacrifices that please God. —HEBREWS 13:16

Are you always cheerful and kind? Are you helpful to others? Or do you complain when someone asks for your help? In the picture on this page Abby and Casey are raking the leaves in their neighbor's yard. What are some of the things you can do to be kind and helpful?

In today's Bible story, let's read together about a kind girl named Rebekah.

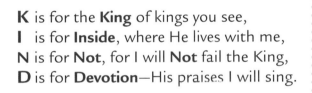

K is for the **King** of kings you see,
I is for **Inside**, where He lives with me,
N is for **Not**, for I will **Not** fail the King,
D is for **Devotion**—His praises I will sing.

Bible Story

Genesis 24:15–20

Abraham's servant had traveled a long time. He was thirsty and so were his ten camels. Finally, he saw a water well. Near the well was a girl named Rebekah. He asked her, "Will you give me some water, please?"

"Yes," Rebekah answered. Then she cheerfully gave the servant some water. "I will give all your camels water too," she said.

Rebekah poured water . . . and poured water . . . and still the camels were thirsty! But Rebekah did not get grumpy or complain; with a happy heart she kept getting water from the well until the camels were no longer thirsty.

Our Together Time

Let's Talk about It!
★ What did Abraham's servant ask Rebekah?
★ What was her answer?
★ What else did Rebekah do?

Share God's Love
That was a lot of camels to give water! Did you know that when you are kind to others and help with a cheerful heart as Rebekah did, you are sharing God's love? Putting away your toys and other things without being told is a way you can be helpful.

See how many toys you can put away
in five minutes.
Ready, set, **GO!**

Prayer
*Dear God, help me to be a cheerful helper
and show kindness to others. Amen.*

The Angry Brother

When you are angry, do not sin. And do not go on being angry all day. —EPHESIANS 4:26

Have you ever been angry with a brother or sister or friend? Esau was angry with his brother, Jacob. Their argument started when Esau realized he had traded his share of their father's property (his birthright) for a bowl of soup. Let's use our together time to make a soup like Jacob's soup. Ask whoever prepares the meals in your family to help you.

JACOB'S SOUP

1 cup dry lentils
1 onion, chopped
3 stalks of celery, diced (optional)
3 carrots, grated
1 pinch of cinnamon

¼ teaspoon of ginger
½ teaspoon of cloves
1 teaspoon cummin (optional)
6 cups of water or broth (chicken, beef, or vegetable)

Pick through the dry lentils to make sure there are no stones or dirt. Rinse and put them in a pot. Put everything else in the same pot and bring it to a boil. Reduce heat and simmer for 1½ hours. Serve with pita bread.

Hint: You can also ask a grownup to buy lentil soup in a can and help you prepare it.

13

Bible Story

Genesis 25:27–34; 27:1–37, 43–44

Esau and Jacob were brothers. Esau was the oldest, which meant when their father's property was divided, Esau would get the most. It was called his "birthright."

One day Jacob made soup while his brother, Esau, went hunting. When Esau came home, he was very, very hungry. "Let me eat some of that soup," Esau said.

"I'll trade you some soup for your birthright," Jacob answered.

Foolishly, Esau agreed to the trade. Their father gave Esau's birthright to Jacob.

Later, Esau thought, *That trade was a big mistake. My birthright is worth more than a bowl of soup!* Esau became very angry. His anger made Jacob afraid. Jacob went far away to his uncle's house, and Jacob did not come home for a long time.

Our Together Time

Let's Talk about It!
★ What did Jacob cook?
★ Why did Esau get angry with Jacob?

Share God's Love

It's okay to be angry, but don't let your anger lead you to do something you know is wrong. Animals get angry in a different way than people—especially people who love Jesus. Try this pretend game to show the difference:

✤ Act like a big, angry bear.
✤ Act like a mad tiger.
✤ Act like an angry monkey.
✤ Now, act like a person who loves Jesus even when you are angry by being kind and thoughtful.

Prayer

Dear Lord, when I am angry, help me to remember to calm down and think about what I'm doing and saying. Amen.

A Happy Heart

A happy heart is like good medicine. —Proverbs 17:22

Have you ever been unhappy and whined when things didn't go your way? Did whining help? Probably not. God knows things won't always go the way we want them to, but He wants us to be happy and joyful because of all He has done for us by sending Jesus as our Savior. Jesus lives in our hearts and brings joy to us. The next time you're tempted to whine about something, sing a song of joy. You can even make up a new song.

17

Bible Story

Exodus 4:29–5:9; 14:29–15:16

When the Israelites heard that God had sent Moses to help them get their freedom from the king of Egypt, they were happy and thanked God for remembering them. But then things didn't go as they expected!

The king would not give them their freedom. Instead, the king made them work harder!

Now they even had to find their own straw to make bricks.

That must have made the Israelites grumpy and unhappy with God and Moses. The Israelites didn't understand that this was all part of God's plan to free them. Later, when God helped the Israelites across the Red Sea to freedom, they were so happy they sang a song to praise God.

Our Together Time

Let's Talk about It!
★ What made the Israelites unhappy?
★ What did they not understand?
★ What did the Israelites do when they were happy?

Share God's Love
When we are grumpy like the Israelites were when things go wrong in our lives, we squish joy from our hearts. Here's a fun way to see how joyful your heart is.

> Get a jar and a handful of beans. Every time you whine or pout or complain, put a bean in the jar. At the end of the week, count your beans and see how you are doing. One bean means you did well. But if you have a lot of beans, you have squished too much joy from your heart and need to work on smiling more and whining less.

Prayer
Dear Lord, I don't want to be a whiner. Help me be happy and cheerful with a heart full of joy. Amen.

God Can Do Anything

"God can do everything!" —LUKE 1:37

God takes care of you every place you go—school, camping, the seashore, visiting friends, home. He takes care of all His people all the time, everywhere. God can do anything! He used a miracle to take care of the Israelites when they left Egypt. Read today's Bible story to see just what an amazing thing God did for them. Moses was so happy, he sang the words below in praise to God. Let's sing them together.

THE SONG OF MOSES

"Are there any gods like you, Lord?
No! There are no gods like you.
You are wonderfully holy.
You are amazingly powerful.
You do great miracles."
—Exodus 15:11 (excerpt)

Bible Story

Exodus 14:5–31

Moses led God's people out of Egypt and right to the banks of a huge sea. There was no way to cross to the other side of the sea. And to make matters worse, the king of Egypt had changed his mind and sent his army to capture them. God's people thought they were trapped. But God was with them. God moved a tall cloud behind them to hide them from the Egyptians. He told Moses to raise his hand over the sea.

God sent a wind that pushed the seawater apart and made a path right through the middle. And guess what? That path was dry. The people didn't even get their sandals muddy as they walked safely across to the other side. Only God can do a miracle like that!

And did you know that when the Egyptian army tried to use the path, the water came back together! And that was the end of the king's army.

Our Together Time

Let's Talk about It!
* Where did Moses lead God's people?
* Who was coming behind them?
* What did God do?

Share God's Love

God takes care of everyone and everything. And He can do anything, like part the Red Sea. Find out just how awesome this miracle was by making a small sea.

A SMALL SEA

Start by filling a small bowl halfway with sand or dirt. Go to the sink and add enough water to cover the sand with about an inch of water over the top. With your hands, try to separate the water into two parts. You can't do it, can you? Now pour the water off the sand. Feel the sand. How long do you think it would take for the sand to get dry?

Prayer
Dear Lord, You helped Your people cross the Red Sea. I know You can take care of me too. Thank You for loving me. Amen.

God Takes Care of Us

My God will use his wonderful riches in Christ Jesus
to give you everything you need. —PHILIPPIANS 4:19

Has your parent or teacher ever asked you to clean up a spill, but then didn't give you any towels to do the job? Probably not. When God asks us to do something, He gives us everything we need to do it. When Moses led God's people out of Egypt and into the desert, there was no water and no food. God provided them a miracle food called "manna."

AMAZING FOOD

No one knows for sure what manna was, but the Bible tells us this:
- Manna came on the ground at night and looked like frost.
- Manna looked like small white seeds.
- Manna tasted like wafers made with honey.

25

Exodus 15:22–17:7

After God's people left Egypt, they began to grumble. "In Egypt we had all the food we wanted," they complained. "Now we will starve in the desert!" God heard them and said He would be sure they had plenty of food. In the evening, He would provide them meat to eat. In the morning, He would give them all the bread they wanted. And He did.

The bread was like nothing God's people had seen before. Thin flakes came on the ground like frost, and the people had to gather it every morning. They didn't know what it was, so they called it manna, which means, "What is it?" Now they had food to eat while they lived in the desert.

Our Together Time

Let's Talk about It!
★ What did the people want?
★ How did they act?
★ What did God send to feed them?

Share God's Love

We don't know what manna was, but we know it was sweet and white. The cookie recipe below might taste a little like manna. Ask a grownup to help you make these cookies. Then share them with others as you tell the story of God's manna miracle.

MANNA COOKIES

½ cup butter	2 teaspoons honey
1 cup sugar	½ teaspoon vanilla
2 eggs	2 cups flour

Cream butter and sugar; add eggs and mix well. Add honey and vanilla. Slowly mix in the flour. Place half teaspoon of dough for each cookie on a baking sheet. Bake at 400 degrees for 8 minutes or until done. Makes three dozen cookies.

Prayer
Dear Lord, I trust You to take care of me.
Thank You for all You do for me. Amen.

God's Book

Your word is like a lamp for my feet and a light for my way.
—Psalm 119:105

Did you know that the most important book in the world is the Bible? The Bible is God's Word. It tells us everything we need to know about God, His Son Jesus, and how to live happy lives. The Bible is divided into the Old Testament and the New Testament. It's actually made up of 66 small books—39 Old Testament books and 27 New Testament books. If you know a song that names the books of the Bible, practice singing it now.

God used men like Moses to write down His Word. In fact, Moses wrote the first five books of the Bible (Genesis, Exodus, Leviticus, Numbers, and Deuteronomy)! To find out more about what God gave Moses, let's read the Bible story together.

29

Exodus 20:2–17; 24:12–18; 31:18

One day God called Moses to the top of a mountain to talk. That's when God gave Moses the Ten Commandments—ten rules—so that God's people would know how He wanted them to live. God wrote the rules on stone with His own finger.

THE TEN COMMANDMENTS

1. God is the only true God. Love and worship only Him.
2. Do not worship or serve any other god or idol.
3. Do not use God's name thoughtlessly.
4. Keep the Sabbath day holy.
5. Honor your father and your mother.
6. Do not murder anyone.
7. Husbands and wives must be faithful to each other.
8. Do not steal.
9. Do not tell lies.
10. Do not wish for someone else's things.

Our Together Time

Let's Talk about It!
★ What did God use to write the Ten Commandments on stone?
★ Why did God give His people rules?
★ Who wrote the first five books of the Bible?

Share God's Love
Isn't it great to know that God loved us so much that He gave us the Bible to help us live happy lives! One way to share God's love is to tell someone why the Bible is the most important book in the world.

For fun, practice saying the
first five books of the Bible.

Ready, set, GO!

Genesis   Exodus   Leviticus   Numbers   Deuteronomy

Prayer
Dear Lord, thank You for the Bible.
Help me to always live by Your rules. Amen.

Try Something New

"The Lord your God will be with you everywhere you go."
—JOSHUA 1:9

Have you ever surprised yourself by being able to do something you didn't think you could do? Perhaps at first it was a little scary, like the first time you tried to ride a bike. Maybe you felt like the little engine who was asked to do a big job. Do you know that story?

One morning, a long line of freight cars asked a big engine to take them over the hill. The big engine didn't think he could do it, and he wouldn't even try. So they asked a little engine if he would try. He was a brave little engine. "I think I can," he said. And he began to pull them up the hill. "I think I can, I think I can," he puffed. Slower and slower he went. Would he make it to the top? Then, all at once, he was over the top, and singing a happy song: "I knew I could, I knew I could."

The next time you are afraid to try something you need to do, trust God to help you and He will give you the courage to do it.

33

Numbers 13:1–14:35

One day Moses sent 12 men to explore the land God was going to give His people. The land had lots of good food, but it also had large walls and people who were like giants. When the 12 men came back, 10 of them said, "We can't go in and take over the land." They were afraid to trust God and try something new. Two men, Joshua and Caleb, said, "Don't worry. God is with us, and He is stronger than any giants." But the people were still afraid to go into the new land. Because the people didn't trust God to help them, they had to wander in the desert for 40 years.

Our Together Time

Let's Talk about It!

* How many of the men who came back wanted to try something new?
* What did the others say?
* What happened because the people did not believe God could help them enter the land He wanted to give them?

Share God's Love

Are you like Joshua and Caleb and trust God to help you do what He needs you to do? Name some things you have had to be brave to try. Here are some ideas to get you thinking:

✤ Going to your first day of school
✤ Learning to swim
✤ Trying new foods

Prayer

Dear Lord, help me to be courageous and remember You are always with me. Amen.

Blind Trust

Happy is the person who trusts the Lord. —PSALM 34:8

Who do you trust? When we trust someone, it means we *believe* that person will do what's best for us—even if we don't always understand how it will happen. When Maddie trusted her mother, she got a fun surprise.

Maddie didn't understand why her mother wanted her to clean her room right then. But she stopped playing and did what her mother asked. Soon she was glad she had, because her mother had a big surprise for her. Maddie's best friend was coming over to swim and spend the night.

And Maddie was all ready to play because she had done what she'd been asked even when she didn't understand why. She had trusted her mother.

In today's Bible story, we see how God gave the Israelites some instructions that didn't seem to make much sense. But when they trusted God and did what He said, an amazing thing happened.

Joshua 6

God wanted His people to capture the city of Jericho. Now Jericho was a city surrounded by huge walls. The people of Jericho closed the big heavy gates in the wall and guarded them so no one could go in or out of the city.

Joshua was the leader of God's people. God told Joshua to tell the people to march around the city of Jericho once a day for six days. The priests were to march in front of the Holy Box with some soldiers in front of them and other soldiers behind the Holy Box.

Then on the seventh day, He wanted them to march around the city seven times. And that's not all. God said the priests were to blow their horns and the people were to give a loud shout, and then the walls would fall down. This may have seemed like a strange way to knock down the city walls, but the people trusted God and did exactly what He asked them to do, and the walls fell down.

Our Together Time

Let's Talk about It!

★ What did God ask His people to do at the walls of Jericho?
★ What happened when the people trusted God and did as He said?

Share God's Love

CRASH!!! How would you have felt if you had been one of the Israelites when those huge walls around Jericho came tumbling down? Stories like this help us know that we can trust God to always do what's best for us. Here's a game about trust.

THE TRUST GAME

You'll need a blindfold and a partner. Wear the blindfold and let your partner guide you through a yard, playground, house, or apartment without running you into anything. Then switch roles. Did you or your partner have trouble trusting each other not to run into anything?

Prayer

Dear Lord, help me to always believe You and trust Your Word even when I don't understand it. Amen.

The Best Help Possible

"Is anything too hard for the Lord? No!" —GENESIS 18:14

Did you know that there is absolutely nothing too hard for God? He can do anything! And here's the best part: He wants to help you when tough times come your way. All you have to do is ask Him. He'll do what's best for you and those you pray for. That's what happened when Joshua and his army had a big, big problem.

Plod, Plod, Plod! That's a fun word to say. Let's say it again: *Plod!* When you plod, you keep going—even when what you are doing is really tough or takes a long time. We say that people running a long race must plod on, putting one foot in front of the other until the race has ended.

Joshua 10:1–14

After Joshua led God's people into the land God had promised them, the Israelite army fought many battles. One day Joshua and his army had been fighting hard, but the battle was not finished. Joshua and his army had not won—not yet.

They needed more time. Joshua needed God's help and said, "Sun, stand still. . . . Moon, stand still. . . ." And the sun and moon "stopped" until Joshua and his army had won the battle. That's what God did for His people.

Our Together Time

Let's Talk about It!

★ Is there anything too hard for God?
★ Why did Joshua need God's help?
★ What did God do for His people?

Share God's Love

Wow! Were you surprised at how God helped Joshua? It's good to know that you can ask God to help you with problems. But you can also ask Him to help others with their problems. Here's something you can make for someone who needs God's help. It's a prayer card.

PRAYER CARD

Find some colorful paper and fold it in half to open like a book. On the outside draw a picture. On the inside write, "I'm praying for you." Sign your name and give it to the person who needs God's help.

Prayer

Dear Lord, thank You for always being there to help me when I need You. I know You can do anything. Amen.

You're a Winner!

We will shout for joy when you succeed. We will raise a flag in the name of our God. —PSALM 20:5

You've probably been a winner more times than you can remember. Everyone has victories where they have worked hard to win a game or overcome a fear or solve a problem. Some victories are large like the first time we spend the night away from home. Some victories are small like when we remember to pick up our toys. One of the best victories of all is the one Jesus gave us over sin—over the wrong things we do.

Long ago the winners of contests, sports, or other such things were given a crown of leaves. Make a victory crown out of paper. Take turns wearing the crown with friends. Whoever is wearing the crown tells a story about a problem he or she overcame.

45

Judges 6:11–24; 6:33–7:8; 7:16–22

Gideon was a warrior God chose to save the people of Israel from their enemy, the Midianites. God sent an angel to tell Gideon what was going to happen and what God wanted him to do. Gideon was pretty sure God had the wrong man because Gideon was the least important member of his family. Gideon was scared. But God told Gideon He would be with him. So Gideon got a big army together. "Too many," said God. Gideon sent thousands of soldiers home. "Too many still," said God, until there were only 300 men.

Then Gideon gave each man a trumpet and a jar with a burning torch inside each jar. Gideon and his men quietly went to the edge of the camp where the enemy was sleeping. His men blew their trumpets, broke the jars, let their torches shine, and shouted, "For the Lord and for Gideon!" It scared the enemy so much they began to fight each other and run away. Gideon won the battle! Hooray, Gideon! Hooray, God!

Our Together Time

Let's Talk about It!

★ What job did God choose Gideon to do?
★ What did Gideon's men do with the trumpets, jars, and torches?
★ What did the enemy do?

Share God's Love

Can you imagine winning a battle without fighting? God helped Gideon be victorious, and He can help you too. What are some things God has helped you overcome? Now name some new challenges you want to be victorious over. Here are some hints:

- Memorizing a Bible verse
- Learning a sport
- Eating your vegetables
- Making a new friend

Prayer

Dear Lord, thank You for giving me victory over sin. And help me remember to ask for Your help when I have a problem. Amen.

God Answers Prayer

"Give thanks to the Lord and pray to him." —1 CHRONICLES 16:8

Did you know that God answers *all* our prayers? Sometimes it may not seem like it, but He does. God's answer might be yes, or it might be no. He might answer us right away, or He might not answer our prayer for a long time. The Bible tells us about Hannah, who wanted something so much that she could hardly think about anything else. When God answered Hannah's prayer, she sang a song of thanks.

HANNAH'S SONG

"The Lord has filled
my heart with joy.
I feel very strong
in the Lord.
I can laugh at my enemies.
I am glad because
you have helped me!"
—1 Samuel 2:1 (excerpt)

49

1 Samuel 1:1–2:2; 2:18–21

Hannah had no children, and that made her very sad. One day she went
to God's Holy Tent, where she asked God to give her a baby son. Eli, the
priest, saw her praying. Hannah told him she was very sad and talking to
God about her troubles. Hannah promised that if God gave her a son,
he would work for God all his life.

God answered Hannah's prayer. She named her son Samuel because Samuel sounds like the Hebrew word for "God heard." Hannah kept her promise, and Samuel worked for God all his life.

Our Together Time

Let's Talk about It!
★ Who prayed and asked God for a child?
★ What did Hannah promise God?

Share God's Love
Have you ever been like Hannah and wanted something so much you could hardly think of anything else? A fun way to see how God answers your prayers is to make a prayer book. Fold some blank pieces of paper in half and staple them together to make a book. Decorate the cover of your prayer book. Inside write your prayers and date them. When God answers your prayer, write a thank-you to God and date it too. You can also draw or paste pictures of the people or things you pray about.

> ### REMEMBER . . .
>
> Sometimes God's answer is yes. Sometimes God's answer is no. And sometimes God's answer is "Not right now." God loves you so much, He will answer with the answer that is the very best for you.

Prayer
Dear Lord, help me to pray often. I'm glad I can talk to You. Amen.

Shhhhhhhhhh!

"Speak, Lord. I am your servant, and I am listening."
—1 SAMUEL 3:10

How well do you listen? Do you pay attention to what your parents and teachers say? Listening carefully is a good way to learn new things. God wants us to listen to His Word so we'll know what He wants us to do. For fun, play the Whispering Game to find out how well you listen.

THE WHISPERING GAME

In the Whispering Game, one person whispers a sentence only once to the person closest to his or her left. That person then whispers the sentence exactly to the person closest to his or her left and so it goes until the last person hears the sentence and says it out loud. Then the person who started the sentence repeats exactly what he or she said. Did the last person hear what the first person said? Try it again. This time the person who was last whispers a new sentence.

1 Samuel 3:1–14

Samuel was a boy who lived in God's Holy Tent. His job was to help Eli, the priest. One night Samuel was asleep when he heard someone call his name. He thought it was Eli. He got up and ran to Eli's bed. "I didn't call you," Eli said. "Go back to bed." So Samuel did.

Soon he heard the voice again. Samuel ran to Eli's bed again. After this happened three times, Eli knew God was calling Samuel. Eli said, "If you hear the voice again, Samuel, say, 'Speak, Lord. I am listening.'" And that is what Samuel did.

Our Together Time

Let's Talk about It!
★ Who did Samuel think called him in the night?
★ What did Eli tell Samuel the third time Samuel woke him up?
★ What happened the fourth time Samuel heard someone call his name?

Share God's Love
What do you think Samuel would say about the noisy world we live in? Our world is so noisy, we don't always listen to the sounds around us. Sit very quietly and listen. What noises do you hear?

✤ A TV
✤ A radio
✤ A computer
✤ What else?

Ask permission to turn off as many sounds as you can. Sit quietly and think about all the wonderful things God has done. Pray and listen. God speaks to us through the Bible. And He speaks so our minds and hearts know what He is saying to us.

Prayer
Dear Lord, teach me to be quiet and listen to what You have to tell me as I read the Bible and pray. Amen.

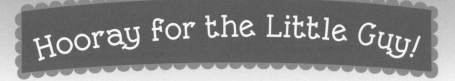

Hooray for the Little Guy!

"Don't be afraid, because I am your God. I will make you strong and will help you." —ISAIAH 41:10

Have you ever been afraid to try something new? Ask God to give you the courage to be brave like the little kite in the following poem.

HOW THE LITTLE KITE LEARNED TO FLY

"I can never do it," the little kite said,
As he looked around at the others high over his head.
"I know I should fall if I tried to fly."
"Try," said the big kite, "only try!
Or I fear you never will learn at all."
But the little kite said, "I'm afraid I'll fall."
. . . .
Then the little kite's paper stirred
   at the sight,
And trembling he shook himself
   free for flight.
First whirling and frightened,
   then braver grown,
Up, up he rose through the air alone.
. . . .
"Oh, how happy I am!"
   the little kite cried,
"And all because I was brave,
   and tried."
—Unknown (excerpt)

57

Bible Story

1 Samuel 17:1–58

David was a shepherd. His job was to look after his father's sheep. Some people may have thought he was just "the little guy." One day his dad sent him to take some food to his brothers who were soldiers in a war. When David got to the battle line, he couldn't believe his eyes! All the soldiers were afraid of a giant named Goliath who was yelling across the valley for God's people to send a warrior out to fight him. No one would go.

Then David said, "I'll go!"

"No, no!" the king said.

But David was full of the courage God had given him. "God will win this battle for me," he said. David gathered five smooth stones and placed them in his pouch. Then with his slingshot in one hand, off he went to fight the giant. The giant was disgusted when he saw that David was just a boy.

David put a stone in the slingshot and whirled it around. The stone flew toward the giant and hit him in the head. The giant toppled to the ground. God had given David the courage to fight Goliath and win the battle.

Our Together Time

Let's Talk about It!
★ Who were the soldiers afraid of?
★ Did David have a big weapon to fight Goliath?
★ How did God help David win the battle?

Share God's Love

Everyone needs courage doing something. David was courageous about facing a big giant. What do you need courage doing? Just for fun . . .

❖ Would it take more courage to jump into a swimming pool or to wear your pajamas backward?
❖ Would you rather say a poem in front of a group or go into a dark room?

With your family, take turns talking about how God gave each of you the courage to do something you had been afraid to do.

Prayer

Dear Lord, I really want to be brave, but sometimes I feel like that little kite. It's hard to try something new. Help me to have courage. Amen.

Friends Forever

A friend loves you all the time. —PROVERBS 17:17

Friends are good to have when you are happy and when you are sad, when you play and when you rest. Did you know that God is always your friend? Here is a poem about friendship. Let's read it together.

FRIENDSHIP

You are my friend
and I am yours.
We play inside
and out of doors.

When I am sad
You hold my hand.
When you are sad
I understand.

Friends forever,
I hope we'll be,
'Til we're at least
A hundred and three.
—Gwen Ellis

Now find out about two best friends in the Bible.

1 Samuel 18:1–16; 20

David and Jonathan were best friends. Jonathan's father, Saul, was king of Israel. Prince Jonathan would have been the next king, but God had chosen David instead. The people loved David. That made King Saul angry and jealous. He was afraid of David and wanted to kill him. Jonathan heard about his father's plan and warned David. Then he helped David run far away where no one could hurt him. Jonathan even gave David his coat to wear.

Our Together Time

Let's Talk about It!
★ Who was Jonathan's best friend?
★ Who was Jonathan's father?
★ Why was King Saul angry and jealous?

Share God's Love
David must have thought about his friend every time he looked at the coat Jonathan gave him. Here's a fun thing to do with your friends to show your friendship.

FRIENDSHIP

Make a friendship bracelet out of a single piece of ribbon, embroidery floss, beautiful thread, or paper chains. Before cutting, carefully measure a piece of ribbon around your friend's wrist so it will fit loosely. Remove it from the wrist, add four inches (or enough to allow you to tie a knot), then cut the ribbon. Now place it back around your friend's wrist, and tie a double-knot so the bracelet fits loosely. Ask a grown-up to cut the ribbon ends near to the knot. *TA-DA!* You made a friendship bracelet!

Prayer
Dear Lord, bless my friends and help us be true friends like Jonathan and David. Amen.

Be Kind

Don't ever stop being kind and truthful. Let kindness and truth show in all you do. —PROVERBS 3:3

Have you ever let a friend go first to play with a new game or toy? Hooray for you! Did you know that when you show kindness it not only makes others happy, it makes God happy too?

When Timmy's mom first told him they were going to help Mrs. Cobb, an elderly lady from their church, he thought it would be boring. But he was wrong! Mrs. Cobb tells wonderful stories and makes yummy pies. Timmy looks forward to spending time with her. He shows kindness by being polite and helping her by doing things like holding the car door open. Being kind is a good way to show God's love.

1 Samuel 31; 2 Samuel 1:1–4; 5:1–4; 9

Long ago David's best friend, Jonathan, died. After David became king, he wanted to show kindess to Jonathan by helping anyone who was still alive in Saul's family. David learned that Jonathan's son Mephibosheth (*mef-ee-bo'-sheth)* was crippled in both feet and living in Lo Debar. David was very kind to Mephibosheth. He treated Jonathan's son as if he were one of his own sons and always let him eat at his table. He also made sure that all of Jonathan's property was returned to Mephibosheth and that the land was farmed, so Mephibosheth would always have food to eat. Mephibosheth lived in Jerusalem, and David took care of him his whole life. David was kind.

Our Together Time

Let's Talk about It!
★ Who is Mephibosheth?
★ How did David show kindness to Mephibosheth?

Share God's Love
If you were Mephibosheth, how would David's kindness make you feel? Are your manners as nice as David's? Here's a fun quiz on kindness.

KINDNESS QUIZ
[Answer True or False]

1. When someone does something nice for you, you should say nothing.
2. When you are finished with dinner, it is kind to help with the dishes.
3. When you receive a gift, you should say, "Thank you."
4. When you see a line of kids waiting their turn for a ride, it is kind to push them out of the way and jump in the ride first.

[1. F / 2. T / 3. T / 4. F]

Prayer
Dear Lord, I want to be a kind child and think of others first. Please help me use good manners. Amen.

Let's Share

"Do for other people the same things you want them to do for you." —MATTHEW 7:12

Tina pulled an apple from her backpack. "Want to share?" she asked Cindy. She did, but Cindy's little brothers wanted some too. What should the girls do? Here's a hint: God wants us to treat others the same way we want to be treated. Read the story below for another hint.

Jennie didn't want to share her toys. Jennie didn't realize how her selfish behavior made her friends feel until one day when she went to Fran's house to play. When Jennie wanted to play with Fran's beautiful dollhouse, Fran wouldn't let her. Jennie didn't like not being allowed to play with the dollhouse. Right then she decided she would treat her friends like she wanted to be treated. Now Jennie and her friends have lots more fun.

69

Bible Story

1 Kings 17:1–16

Times were hard in Israel. The people had not been faithful to God and He was not sending them rain. So God put Elijah near a stream where he would have water to drink and where birds fed him bread and meat. But after a while the stream dried up. Then God told Elijah to go to a certain woman and ask her for food.

Elijah went and asked. The woman said she only had enough flour and oil for one more meal for her son and herself, and then they would die of hunger. Elijah told her to cook for him first and she would be all right. Because she had a sharing heart, she did what Elijah asked and cooked him a piece of bread. Guess what? God made her food last so that the woman, her son, and Elijah would eat until once again there was food in the land.

Our Together Time

Let's Talk about It!
★ What did God tell Elijah to do?
★ What did the woman do to help Elijah?
★ What did God provide for the woman, her son, and Elijah?

Share God's Love

When the woman gave Elijah food, she was doing something God wants us all to do: She was sharing! She was treating Elijah the same way she'd want to be treated.

Here's a fun way to start thinking about things you can share. Start by drawing a heart shape on a piece of paper. Next draw lines across it to divide it into four parts. In each part, draw a picture of something that is hard for you to share but that you will begin sharing to please God. Talk with your family about ways you can begin sharing. Then decide what you will do the next time you are asked to share. Now you have a sharing heart.

Prayer
Dear God, help me learn to share with others
as You want me to. Amen.

Fire from Heaven

Pray with all kinds of prayers, and ask for everything you need.
—EPHESIANS 6:18

Every day you talk to lots of people—your family, friends, teachers, and maybe even your teddy bear. But did you know that God wants you to talk to Him every day too? When you talk to God, it's called prayer. And you can talk to Him anytime, anywhere. God can help us with our problems, big or small—all we need to do is ask. We don't need to yell or scream.

*Julius wanted a bear.
He wanted it NOW!
He wouldn't share.
He yelled, he stomped,
and threw a fit.
In a loud voice said,
"I deserve it!"*

*Mom wasn't pleased.
God was unhappy too.
His sister got the bear.
And she said, "Thank you!"*
—Laura Minchew

In today's Bible story, find out what mighty thing happened when Elijah talked to God.

1 Kings 18:1, 15–46

After about three years with no rain, the people of Israel were desperate for water. So all 450 prophets who prayed to the false god called Baal met Elijah—a prophet of the only real God—on a mountaintop. The group of prophets built an altar to Baal, placed wood on it, and then placed an offering of meat on top of the wood. Elijah did the same, but his altar was to God.

The prophets yelled and screamed from morning until evening as they begged Baal to answer them and send fire. No answer came. No fire came. (This is because Baal is not a god. There is only one God. Do you know who it is?)

Now it was Elijah's turn. He had people pour water on the wood and the offering of meat until the altar was soaked. The people knew it was too wet for a fire to light. Next Elijah asked the real God to answer by sending fire to burn the wet offering! Just like that, God sent fire that burned up the entire altar. Wow! God had answered Elijah's prayer and proved that He was the real God.

Our Together Time

Let's Talk about It!
★ How long had the people of Israel been without rain?
★ What did the prophets of the false god Baal do?
★ What did Elijah do when it was his turn?

Share God's Love
Isn't it good to know that you can talk to God about anything? He's interested in everything you think and feel. Did something exciting happen to you? Tell God. We all have good days and not-so-good days! What kind of day is it when . . .

✤You fall down in a mud puddle?
✤You learn something new?
✤You scrape your knee?
✤You go for a swim in a pool full of Jell-O?

Prayer
Dear God, I know You are a mighty God who can do anything. That is why I pray to You. Thank You for hearing my prayers. Amen.

An Honest Person

"Tell each other the truth." —Zechariah 8:16

Do you always tell the truth and try to do the right thing? Would you return a wallet you found—even if it had money in it? Sometimes it might seem that telling lies and not being honest is easier than telling the truth. But God wants us to tell the truth.

Did you know that one of the presidents of the United States was such an honest person he was called "Honest Abe"? His real name was Abraham Lincoln. It is believed that he got this nickname when he worked as a clerk in a store as a young man. One day he gave a customer incorrect change. When he discovered his mistake, Lincoln walked a long way to give the person the right change.

In today's Bible story, we'll see how lies led to some really bad things.

1 Kings 21–22:39

One day King Ahab went to his neighbor, Naboth, and asked for his land to plant a vegetable garden. Naboth said, "No." It made the king very angry. When he told his wife, Queen Jezebel, what had happened, she got very angry too.

So the queen made a plan that would help them get Naboth's land. At that time, speaking badly against God or the king was against the law. Queen Jezebel got some people to say that Naboth had said bad things about God and the king.

The king and queen knew it was a lie, but they let Naboth be killed for something he didn't do, just to get his land.

Later, King Ahab and Queen Jezebel both died terrible deaths because of all the lies and evil things they had done.

Our Together Time

Let's Talk about It!
★ What did King Ahab and Queen Jezebel want?
★ What did they do to get it?
★ What happened to King Ahab and Queen Jezebel?

Share God's Love
Ugh! That story didn't have a happy ending. But God wants us to know that lies and wrongdoing can hurt others and the liars and wrongdoers too. Share God's love by always telling the truth and being honest with everyone you meet. If you have told a lie, ask for forgiveness from the person you lied to. Play this game to see how good you are at knowing whether or not someone is telling a lie.

> ### THE TRUTH GAME
>
> Take turns being the speaker. The speaker can choose to tell the truth or a lie. The rest of the people in the room guess whether the speaker was telling the truth or a lie. Who guessed right the most often?

Prayer
Dear Lord, help me to always tell the truth. Amen.

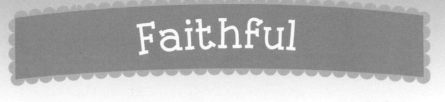

Faithful

"If you are faithful, I will give you the crown of life."
—REVELATION 2:10

In Yellowstone Park there is an amazing feature called Old Faithful Geyser. Perhaps you've seen it. It is a hole in the ground that shoots hot water into the air every 60 to 90 minutes. No one knows how long the geyser has been doing this or when it was discovered, but it got its name in 1879 because of how it faithfully spouted hot water, which it's still doing today.

You can see Old Faithful for yourself. Ask a grownup to help you search the Internet for Yellowstone Park's Web site. Within the park menu, click on Old Faithful.

In today's Bible story, we'll read about Elijah, one of God's faithful followers. God wants us to be faithful by living for Him every day too.

2 Kings 2:1–12

Elijah was a faithful servant of God. He stayed true to God even though he was threatened by a wicked queen and had to hide out in the desert. As he got older, Elijah continued to serve God faithfully. He trained his helper Elisha to do the same thing. Elisha went everywhere with Elijah until one day something amazing happened.

Fiery horses and a chariot of fire came down from heaven, and—
WHOOSH!—a whirlwind carried Elijah straight up to heaven. He was
faithful to God right to the end, and God was faithful to bring Elijah
right up to heaven to be with Him forever.

Let's Talk about It!
★ What kind of a servant of God was Elijah?
★ Where did Elijah go in the whirlwind?

Share God's Love
Wow! Isn't it amazing how God took Elijah to heaven? And it's good to know that one day we, too, can go to heaven by being God's faithful followers. How faithful are you? Try this quiz.

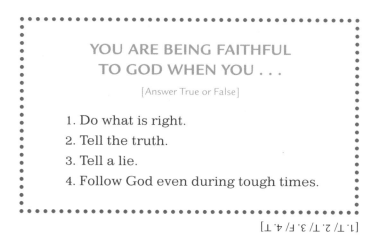

YOU ARE BEING FAITHFUL
TO GOD WHEN YOU . . .

[Answer True or False]

1. Do what is right.
2. Tell the truth.
3. Tell a lie.
4. Follow God even during tough times.

[1. T / 2. T / 3. F / 4. T]

Prayer
Dear Lord, I'm just learning about being faithful. Help me be loyal, true, and dependable in everything I do. Amen.

God Provides

Praise the Lord, day by day. God our Savior helps us.
—PSALM 68:19

How many names do you have? Think about it. You have your given first name and maybe a middle name. You have a last name and maybe a nickname. You might be called son or daughter, niece or nephew, grandson or granddaughter. Sometimes what you are called tells something about you.

Did you know that God has several names that describe Him too? One of God's names means "The Lord provides." The Lord gives us what we need. Sometimes He does that by providing others to help us. In today's Bible story, we'll see how God used Elisha to provide the help someone needed.

God has sent people to help you too. These people might be called mom, dad, grandma, grandpa, aunt, uncle, brother, sister, teacher, or friend. Quick, name as many people as you can who God has sent to help you. **Ready, set, GO!**

85

2 Kings 4:1–7

A woman went to Elisha, the prophet of God, for help. She was very upset. Her husband had died, and he owed another man a lot of money. That man was going to take the woman's two sons and make them slaves, unless she could pay what her husband owed him. Elisha asked the woman what she had in her house. The woman said, "I have nothing but a small pot of oil."

Elisha told her to get all the empty jars she could borrow from her neighbors. "Take your small pot of oil and begin pouring it into all the empty jars," Elisha told her. The woman did as he said. She poured and poured and poured until every jar was full. Then the woman took the jars and sold the oil to pay her debt. Now her sons got to stay at home with her, and they had plenty of money to live on. Hooray! God had provided for her.

Our Together Time

Let's Talk about It!
★ What was the woman's problem?
★ What did Elisha tell her to do?
★ What did God do for her and her sons?

Share God's Love

A pot of oil! Who would have known that was all the woman and her sons needed? But God knew, and He sent Elisha to help her. Today God still sends people to help others. God sends people like you to provide what others need. Sometimes what a person needs is something as small as someone to open a door. Sometimes it's very big, like someone to adopt a child or bring food to those who are hungry. You never know how God will use you to help others, but you can be sure He will.

> Name five ways God has used you
> and your family to help others.

Prayer
Dear Lord, I'm glad You provide for my needs. Please use me to help others whenever I can. Amen.

Achoo!

I praise you because you made me in an amazing and wonderful way. —Psalm 139:14

God created sneezes to protect us. There is a wonderful story in the Bible about a little boy who sneezed a big sneeze. Who do you suppose it was? And why was a sneeze so important? Read the Bible story on the next page to find out.

FACTS ABOUT SNEEZES

- You sneeze to clear your breathing passages.
- Your whole body gets into it? Your nose tickles, your brain tells you to sneeze, and your muscles get ready for the big event.
- Most people close their eyes when they sneeze. Do you?
- You sneeze at the smell of pepper.
- The speed of a sneeze can be more than 100 miles per hour!

Bible Story

2 Kings 4:8–37

Elisha often stayed with a Shunammite woman, her husband, and their young son. The family had even built a special room for Elisha on the roof of their house.

One day, the little boy became sick when he went out in the field where his father was harvesting grain. They took the little boy home, but there was nothing anyone could do. The little boy died. The Shunammite woman placed the boy on Elisha's bed. She hurried to get Elisha to bring him to help her little boy. Elisha went with the lady back to her house and prayed. Then all of a sudden, *"Achoo!"* The little boy sneezed. Then he sneezed six more times and opened his eyes. It was a miracle. God had brought the little boy back to life.

Our Together Time

Let's Talk about It!
★ What happened to the little boy?
★ What did God do when Elisha prayed for the little boy?

Share God's Love
Has anyone ever said, "God bless you!" when you sneezed? Many people do, and it's always a good way to share God's love, because it's like saying a prayer for someone.

FUNNY SNEEZES

On a piece of paper, draw as many round circles as there are people in your family. Put eyes on each of the circles. Now think about how each person sneezes. Draw a mouth and nose to show that person's sneeze. How funny does it look? Did you remember to draw a picture of yourself?

Prayer
Dear Lord, You are the One who gave me my breath and my sneezes. Thank You for my amazing body. Amen.

The Borrowed Ax

Do not be interested only in your own life, but
be interested in the lives of others. —PHILIPPIANS 2:4

How do you feel when you lose something? Are you sad? What if you
had borrowed what you lost from a friend? Now the friend it belonged
to will be sad too. When we borrow something, we should take care
of it as if it were the most important thing we ever had—whether it is
something very small or very big, whether it cost a lot of money or none
at all. In the Bible story on the next page, a man was
very sad when he lost something he had borrowed.
See what God's prophet Elisha did to
help the man.

2 Kings 6:1–7

Long ago work tools were made by hand, and tools were expensive and rare. One day some prophets were chopping down trees with heavy axes to build them a place to live. While they were working, a man gave a strong chop to a tree with an ax. When he did that, the heavy iron axhead flew off the handle and went right into the water. It quickly sank.

"Oh no," said the man, "I borrowed that ax." He was sad. He wouldn't be able to return the ax to its owner.

Elisha, the prophet, was there. He asked, "Where did it fall?" The man showed him. Elisha cut a stick and threw it into the water, and the heavy iron axhead floated to the surface. The man who lost it picked it up. It was a miracle.

Our Together Time

Let's Talk about It!
* ★ What happened to one man's ax while chopping down trees?
* ★ What did Elisha do?
* ★ What floated to the water's surface?

Share God's Love
Do you think the axhead would have been able to float to the top without Elisha's help? Try this experiment.

THE SINKING PENNY

You'll need a clear glass or plastic cup, clear water, and a penny. Fill the glass three-quarters full of water. Place the glass where everyone can see it. Drop the penny in the glass. Did the penny float? An axhead is much heavier than a penny. Share God's love by telling someone about the amazing miracle of the floating axhead.

Prayer
Dear Lord, help me take care of anything I borrow from others as if it were my own. I want to take good care of everything I use. Thank You, Lord. Amen.

I Choose You

"Who knows, you may have been chosen queen for just such a time as this." —ESTHER 4:14

Have you ever been chosen to do something special? It can be lots of fun, but sometimes it can be a little scary too. Maybe you were chosen to help a teacher, or tell about a trip you made, or sing a song, or be on a team to play a game. Let's read together the Bible story on the next page and find out about a beautiful, young queen who was chosen by God for a very big job. She lived in Persia, which today we know as Iran. If you want to know where that is, ask someone to help you find it on a map.

97

Esther 1–9

Esther was an ordinary girl living in Persia. Then God chose her for an extraordinary job. First she became queen of the land. But after she was queen, one of the king's men wanted to do away with all God's people.

Esther's cousin Mordecai came to her. He knew that God could use Esther to save God's people. He told her, "It could be that God has made you queen for just this time."

What Esther did next was very courageous. Even though the king could have killed her, she went to the king and asked him to save her people. The king did what she asked. Yea, Esther!

Our Together Time

Let's Talk about It!
★ Where did Esther live?
★ What did God choose her to do?
★ What happened when she did what God asked?

Share God's Love

God chooses people to get His work done. You can share God's love by helping to do His work on earth. What are some ways you can help God with His work?

✤ Maybe you could give some of your toys to someone who doesn't have any.
✤ Maybe there is something you could do to help your parents, your grandparents, and even your brothers and sisters.

What else can you think of that can help God with His work? Ask a grownup to help you make a plan. Then do the work. You'll be glad you did.

Prayer
Dear Lord, help me to think of things I can do to be Your helper. Amen.

The Right Time

There is a right time for everything. —ECCLESIASTES 3:1

When you have choices to make, do you ever have a hard time deciding what's most important? Everything has an order—even your shoes and socks. What would happen if you put on your shoes and then your socks? That wouldn't work, would it? So the best choice is to put on your socks and then your shoes. Now, if you had to choose between watching your favorite TV program or doing your homework, which one should you do first? The Bible tells us that there is a right time for everything God has given us to do.

BEDTIME ORDER

For fun, number these bedtime things in the best order.

___Get in bed.
___Have sweet dreams.
___Brush your teeth.
___Eat a snack.
___Say your prayers.

Ecclesiastes 3:1–8

A wise man said in the Bible that there is a right time for everything in life. Some things we can't choose, such as when to be born. But other things we can choose, such as when to be silent and when to speak or when to hug and when not to hug or when to be happy and when to be sad. God wants us to make good choices about our time and to let Him take care of those things we can't make happen or fix or change. He is in control of everything.

Our Together Time

Let's Talk about It!
★ What does the Bible say about the time for things?
★ What kind of choices does God want us to make?

Share God's Love
Isn't it great that there is a time for everything! There's a time to be awake and a time to go to sleep. There is a time to go places and a time to stay home. There is a time to work and a time to play.

> ### IT'S TIME
>
> Draw some clocks for your room. These can be clocks with hands or digital clocks. Each clock should show the time you or your family do something. Write over your clock what you do at this time. Is it eat dinner? Go to church? Go to bed? Make as many clocks as you need.

Prayer
Dear Lord, please help my family and me to make good choices about what we are doing. Amen.

God's Angels
Watch Over You

"Don't think these little children are worth nothing. I tell you that they have angels in heaven who are always with my Father in heaven." —MATTHEW 18:10

Did you know that God sends His angels to watch over us? God promises in the Bible that He will put His angels in charge of you. Let's read together His promise below.

He has put his angels in charge of you.
They will watch over you wherever you go. . . .
The Lord says, "If someone loves me,
*   I will save him.*
I will protect those who know me.
They will call to me, and I will
*   answer them.*
I will be with them in trouble.
I will rescue them and
*   honor them.*
I will give them a long,
*   full life.*
They will see how I can save."
—Psalm 91:11, 14–16

Now check out today's Bible story to see how God's angel helped Daniel.

Daniel 6:11–28

Daniel was a man who loved God with all his heart. He prayed to God three times a day. The king was planning to put Daniel in charge of the whole kingdom. This made some leaders jealous, and they tricked the king into throwing Daniel into a hungry lions' den.

But God sent His angel to take care of Daniel. The angel closed the lions' jaws so they couldn't bite Daniel.

In the morning, the king had Daniel removed from the lions' den. Daniel was not hurt at all, because he had trusted in God.

Our Together Time

Let's Talk about It!
★ What happened to Daniel?
★ Who did God send to help Daniel?

Share God's Love
To share God's love, make paper angels for your family and friends and tell them how God's angels are watching over us. For each angel, you'll need two round coffee filters, glue, coloring crayons, and a little stiff paper or felt. Ask a grownup to help.

1. **Wings:** Fold one filter in half and put to the side.
2. **Angel's body:** Fold the second filter in half, then fold the sides back so the edges meet in the center to form a cone shape. Glue together. With the first filter's folded edge at the top, glue it to the back of the cone—so that the top of the cone is below the center point of the wings.
3. **Angel's face:** Cut a small circle from stiff paper or felt and draw a face on it. Glue to the top of the cone.

Prayer
Dear Lord, thank You for sending angels to watch over me. Even though I may not see them, I know they are there because Your Word tells me so. Amen.

I Will Obey

Children, obey your parents in all things.
This pleases the Lord. —COLOSSIANS 3:20

Have your parents ever asked you to do something you really didn't want to do? Did you do it anyway just because they asked you? If so, good for you! That was obeying. Here's a fun way to see what else you know about obeying.

THE FUN OBEYING QUIZ
[Answer True or False]

1. When children disobey, they usually get ice cream.
2. Grownups do not have to follow the rules.
3. God wants children to obey their parents.
4. God wants everyone to obey Him.
5. Rules are made to keep us all safe.

[1. F / 2. F / 3. T / 4. T / 5. T]

109

Bible Story

Jonah 1–3:10

God told Jonah to go to Nineveh and preach to the people. But Jonah didn't like those people, so he disobeyed God and got on a ship going the opposite direction from Nineveh. At sea, a terrible storm was about to sink the ship. Everyone was afraid.

Jonah told the sailors to throw him overboard, and the storm would stop. That's what they did, and the storm did stop! A large fish quickly swallowed Jonah.

God let Jonah stay in the belly of that stinky old fish for three days, until Jonah prayed to Him saying he would obey.

Then that fish spit Jonah up on dry land. And Jonah went straight to Nineveh and preached to the people.

Our Together Time

Let's Talk about It!
* ★ Why did Jonah choose not to obey God?
* ★ What did Jonah do?
* ★ What made Jonah change his mind about obeying God?

Share God's Love

Sometimes we're like Jonah; we don't want to do what God asks. But God always has a good reason for everything. He knows everything about you. He knows what's best. Obeying God is a great way to show that you love Him. Now for fun try this game that can only be won by obeying.

> ### SIMON SAYS
>
> To play, one person is Simon or "it." Simon stands in front of everyone. No one moves until Simon tells him or her what to do. When Simon gives a command (like "Simon says turn in a circle"), everyone must follow the command. But if Simon gives a command (like "turn in a circle") without saying "Simon says," no one should move—and if someone does move, that person is out. The last person still in the game is the most obedient.

Prayer
Dear God, help me to obey—even when I don't want to. Amen.

God's Family

The Father has loved us so much . . . that we
are called children of God. —1 JOHN 3:1

There are all kinds of families. How would you describe your family?
Families are important to God. They are so important to Him that even
though He could have sent His Son to earth as a grown man, He didn't.
He sent Jesus as a little baby to be part of an earthly family with Mary as
His mother and Joseph as His father.

Did you know that anyone who believes in
Jesus can be part of God's family? Wow!
That's one big family! Think of everyone
you're related to when you join God's
family. You could count for hours,
days, months, even
years, and still
not name
them all!

Luke 1:26–2:52; John 19:25–27; Matthew 1:18–2:23

When God was ready to send His Son to the world, He chose Mary and Joseph, a couple who were about to get married. He sent an angel to tell Mary that she was going to have a baby. Then God sent an angel to talk to Joseph and tell him he should make a home for Mary and the baby. Jesus was born in Bethlehem, where shepherds and wise men came to honor Him.

Later Jesus lived in Nazareth where Mary and Joseph took care of Him until He was grown. And Jesus obeyed them as His parents. He never forgot them and the safe place they had made for Him to live. Even as He was dying on the Cross, Jesus was thinking about His mother.

Our Together Time

Let's Talk about It!
★ Who were Jesus' parents on earth?
★ How did Jesus act toward Mary and Joseph?

Share God's Love
Isn't it good to know that you can be part of God's family? For fun make a family tree showing some of the people from the Bible who are also children of God. Remember to include yourself. Here's an example:

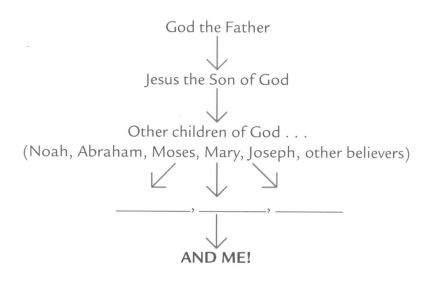

God the Father

Jesus the Son of God

Other children of God . . .
(Noah, Abraham, Moses, Mary, Joseph, other believers)

_____, _____, _____

AND ME!

Prayer
Dear Lord, thank You for making a great big family of those who believe, and inviting us all to be a part of Your family. Amen.

Jesus' Birthday

Thanks be to God for his gift that is too wonderful to explain.
—2 CORINTHIANS 9:15

When you think about Christmas, do you think about trees and presents? Did you know that Christmas is the time when many Christians celebrate the birth of Jesus? That's right, they're having a big birthday party for Jesus! Long ago, when Jesus was born, some shepherds got the news from a messenger of God, an angel! We still sing about what the angels said today. Sing the song below.

ANGELS WE HAVE
HEARD ON HIGH

Come to Bethlehem and see
Him Whose birth the angels sing,
Come, adore on bended knee,
Christ the Lord, the newborn King.
—James Chadwick (excerpt)

In today's Bible story, find out what the shepherds thought when they first saw the angel and how they found the baby Jesus.

117

Bible Story

Luke 2:8–20

The best news in the whole world came to shepherds who were watching over their sheep. Suddenly, an angel in a bright light appeared to tell them something wonderful. When the shepherds first saw the angel, they were afraid.

"Don't be afraid," the angel said. "I have good news for you. Your Savior was born in Bethlehem tonight. He's Christ the Lord. You will find Him lying in a feeding box."

Then a very large group of angels joined the first angel. They all were praising God. When the angels went back to heaven, the shepherds went to Bethlehem and found Mary and Joseph and saw the baby lying in a feeding box. It was just as the angel had told them.

Our Together Time

Let's Talk about It!
★ Who heard the news of Jesus' birth while watching sheep?
★ Who told them?

Share God's Love
Christmas is one of the best times of the year to share God's love. Make Christmas cards to share with your family and friends. On your cards, draw pictures of

❖ angels,
❖ the shepherds,
❖ baby Jesus.

Your cards will tell others about the good news of Jesus' birth. If others are making cards with you, take turns talking about what each of you might have thought if you had been one of the shepherds and an angel appeared before you.

Prayer
Dear Jesus, thank You for coming to be my Savior. I love You. Amen.

God's Best Promise Comes True

"For God loved the world so much that he gave his only Son.
God gave his Son so that whoever believes in him
may not be lost, but have eternal life." —JOHN 3:16

Do you keep your promises? God keeps His. When God says something will happen, it will happen. God's best promise was that He would send His Son, Jesus, to us. He told us how Jesus would come to earth and what Jesus would do here. Every promise came true.

WHAT GOD PROMISED

- Jesus would be born in Bethlehem (Micah 5:2).
- Jesus would ride into Jerusalem on the colt of a donkey (Zechariah 9:9).
- Jesus would die for our sins (Isaiah 53:4–5).

Luke 2:1–7; 19:29–38; Matthew 27:35, 45–50

Mary and Joseph lived in Nazareth. Just before it was time for Jesus to be born, they had to go to Bethlehem. While they were there, Jesus was born—just as God had promised.

When Jesus was a grownup, He rode the colt of a donkey into Jerusalem. Crowds of His followers said, "God bless the king who comes in the name of the Lord!"

Later, Jesus was arrested and nailed to a cross where He died for our sins.

Our Together Time

Let's Talk about It!
★ Where did Mary and Joseph live?
★ Where did God say Jesus would be born?
★ What happens when God makes a promise?

Share God's Love

Here's a fun way to share God's love. Make a promise book and write promises from the Bible in it. To get started look at God's promises in these Bible verses and write them down in your book.

John 3:16

1 John 1:9

Philippians 2:12

Proverbs 3:6

Joshua 1:9

Psalm 46:1

James 5:16

James 1:5

Prayer
Dear Lord, thank You for keeping Your promises. Help me learn more about You and Your promises. Amen.

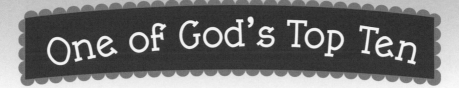

One of God's Top Ten

Children, obey your parents the way the Lord wants.
This is the right thing to do. —EPHESIANS 6:1

Did you know that honoring your parents is one of God's top ten rules? So what does "honoring" mean? The answer is simple: You honor your parents when you do what they ask, follow the rules they make, and behave well—even when your parents are not in the room.

How well do you honor your parents? Answer the following questions yes or no:

1. Do you enjoy spending time with your parents?
2. Do you do what your parents ask you to do?
3. Do you say "please" and "thank you" to your parents and others?

If you answered every question "YES!" you are doing a great job of honoring your parents. If you answered any question "no," ask your parents what you can do to change that "no" into a "YES!"

125

Luke 2:41–52

When Jesus was 12 years old, He went with His parents to the Temple in Jerusalem. Soon it was time to go home to Nazareth. Everyone packed up and left.

At first Mary and Joseph thought Jesus was traveling with some of their family and friends. When they realized Jesus wasn't in the group, they went back to Jerusalem where they found Jesus talking with some religious teachers in the Temple just as if He was one of them.

When Mary and Joseph told Jesus it was time to go, He honored them by respectfully doing what they asked. He left the teachers and went home with Mary and Joseph. There He continued to learn and grow, to obey His parents, and to please God in all that He did.

Our Together Time

Let's Talk about It!
★ What is God's rule about parents?
★ What was Jesus doing in the Temple?
★ How did Jesus honor His parents?

Share God's Love
Think about it! Jesus was once a kid like you with earthly parents. It's hard to imagine, isn't it? Honoring your parents is an easy way to be even more like Jesus. Do you know your parents' favorite words? They are:

"I LOVE YOU!"

Every mom and every dad likes to hear those words. Can you say them now and share a hug?

Prayer
Dear God, please help me be the child You want me to be and honor my parents. Amen.

Say No to Temptation

And now he [Jesus] can help those who are tempted . . . because he himself suffered and was tempted. —HEBREWS 2:18

When we are tempted, it is as if someone is tapping us on the shoulder to get us to do something we know we shouldn't do. If you've ever wanted to sneak a yummy cookie when you were told to wait, you've been tempted. If you've ever wanted to play with your friends when you were told to clean your room, you've been tempted.

It's no surprise that *everyone* is tempted. Even Jesus was tempted. See today's Bible story and find out how. The important thing is to turn away from temptation and DO THE RIGHT THING!

Matthew 4:1–11

When Jesus was tempted, He was out in the desert all alone. Jesus was very hungry and tired when Satan came to tempt Him to do some things that were wrong.

First Satan told Jesus to "turn these rocks into bread." But Jesus had studied God's Word, so He remembered what He had learned from the Scriptures. He said, "A person doesn't live just by eating bread. A person lives by doing everything the Lord says."

"Jump down from the top of the Temple. God's angels will catch you," said Satan. Jesus answered, "The Scriptures also say, 'Do not test God.'"

Then Satan took Jesus to the top of a tall mountain and showed Him all the kingdoms of the world. "Bow down and give honor to me, and I will give you all these things," said Satan. But Jesus said, "Go away from Me! It is written in the Scriptures, 'You must worship only the Lord God.'" And Satan left.

Our Together Time

Let's Talk about It!
★ How was Jesus feeling when Satan came to Him?
★ Did Jesus do the right or the wrong thing?

Share God's Love
Like Jesus, you too can say "No!" to temptation. Here's a fun way to help you remember:

> Say, "No! No! No!" loud and clear,
> Don't pretend that you aren't here.
> You know right is right and wrong is wrong.
> Hear it, believe it, be strong.
> Throw out temptation as you should.
> Then bless the Lord for all that's good.
> —June Ford

Now share God's love with your family and friends by telling about three times you've said "No!" to temptation.

Prayer
Dear God, sometimes it is hard to do what is right. Please help me say no to temptation and to do the right thing. Amen.

When You're Sick

The prayer that is said with faith will make the sick person well. The Lord will heal him. —James 5:15

Have you ever been sick? Yuck! It's no fun, is it? But we can ask Jesus today to heal us when we are sick. He knows what we need. He knows the doctors and medicines that will help us get well. He gives us family and friends who take care of us. He puts foods like fruits, vegetables, and grains on earth for us to eat. He gives us lots of ways to exercise like walking, running, jumping, and climbing. He provides us a way to relax our body through sleep. So even though we may not see Jesus, He can heal us. Read today's Bible story and see how Jesus healed a child He never saw.

> Pretend that someone in your family is sick. It could be Mom, Dad, your brother or sister— even one of your toys. What do you need to do to take care of that person?

Bible Story

John 4:46–53

One day at exactly one o'clock in the afternoon, an important man in the government begged Jesus to come heal his son. The boy was very, very sick and in a different town. Jesus knew He didn't need to go there. He told the father, "Go home. Your son will live." The man believed Jesus and went home.

On the man's way home, his servants met him and told him his son was well. The father asked what time his son began to get well. The servants said, "Your son's fever went away at one o'clock yesterday." The father knew that was the exact time Jesus had said, "Your son will live." Now not only did the man believe in Jesus, all the people in his house believed in Jesus too.

Our Together Time

Let's Talk about It!
★ What did Jesus do when the man asked Him to heal his son?
★ Who believed in Jesus?

Share God's Love
No one likes to be sick, but it's good to know that Jesus can help us even if we can't see Him! For a little fun, see how well you know what to do to stay healthy.

A HEALTH QUIZ

[Answer True or False]

To keep your body strong and healthy . . .

1. Eat candy and cookies three times a day.
2. Go to bed on time to let your body rest.
3. Put ice cream on your vegetables.
4. Exercise every day.
5. Ride your bike or play a game outside.
6. Never ever brush your teeth.

[1. F/ 2. T/ 3. F/ 4. T/ 5. T/ 6. F]

Prayer
*Dear Lord, help me eat right and sleep well
so that I can stay well. Amen.*

Being a Helper

Trust the Lord and do good. —PSALM 37:3

You can be a helper whether you are very, very young or very, very old. Think of some of the many ways you can be a helper. In the story below, Laura thought of a way to be a big help to her mother.

Laura was a new big sister. One evening when her mother was making dinner, Laura thought of a way she could help. She got on the floor beside her baby brother and began to talk to him, making him smile and kick his feet. She kept him busy until dinner was ready.

"Thanks for being such a good helper, Laura!" her mother said.

Laura really liked being a helper.

God wants you to be a helper too. In today's Bible story, find out how a little boy helped Jesus.

137

Bible Story

John 6:1–14; Matthew 14:13–21

One day a crowd of people followed Jesus to see His miracles and hear Him teach about God's love. By the time they reached Jesus, it was late in the day, and there were more than 5,000 hungry people. But there was no food, except for five small loaves of bread and two small fish that a boy had brought with him. The boy gave his bread and fish to Jesus' helpers.

Jesus thanked God for the boy's food and gave everyone there as much to eat as they wanted. It was a miracle. There were even 12 baskets of food left over!

Our Together Time

Let's Talk about It!
* How was the boy a helper?
* What was in the boy's lunch?
* What did Jesus do?

Share God's Love
You can be a good helper by making bread and fish sandwiches for lunch. One type of bread and fish sandwich is called a tuna fish sandwich. Ask a grownup to help you prepare tuna fish sandwiches for everyone in your home. Before you eat, say a prayer thanking God for the food.

> *God is great.*
> *God is good.*
> *Let us thank Him*
> *For our food.*
> —Traditional

While you eat the sandwiches, tell them the story of how Jesus fed more than 5,000 people.

Prayer
Dear Lord, I want to help others. Please show me ways that I can be helpful. Amen.

Don't Be Afraid

I go to bed and sleep in peace. Lord, only you keep me safe.
—PSALM 4:8

What makes you afraid? Strange noises? Dark rooms? New places?
Everyone is afraid of something. In today's Bible story, we'll even see how
Jesus' helpers were afraid. But did you know that most of the things we
are afraid of are not real or don't happen, like when we find out a strange
noise was only a tree limb scraping the side of the house? Below is a
Bible verse that you can memorize and say the next time you are afraid.

*When I am afraid,
I will trust you.*
—Psalm 56:3

141

Bible Story

Mark 6:45–53

One day Jesus asked His helpers to go to a town across the lake. He said He would join them later. The men did as Jesus asked and got into a boat and set out across the lake. A strong wind came up. The wind blew fiercely. The men were very afraid! They rowed harder and harder toward the shore, but the wind kept pushing them back into the lake. Then they saw something that scared them even more. A man was walking on the water toward them! Then the man called out, "Don't be afraid." And they realized it was Jesus walking toward them. Jesus got into their boat, and suddenly the wind became calm. The helpers were amazed. Everything was all right because Jesus was with them.

Our Together Time

Let's Talk about It!
★ What made Jesus' helpers afraid?
★ What did Jesus do?

Share God's Love
Did you know that the Bible mentions fear more than 350 times? That's a lot of being scared. But the important thing to realize is that we know Jesus is always close by no matter what is happening.

> ### FOR FUN, ACT OUT THE STORY
>
> With your family, act out the story of the men in the boat and Jesus walking to them on the water. Pretend the floor or ground is water. The boat could be made of pillows or chairs. When you have finished your play, all together say Psalm 56:3, "When I am afraid, I will trust you." Give everyone a hug.

Prayer
Dear Lord, sometimes I am afraid. Help me know that You are always with me and to ask for Your help when I'm afraid. Amen.

Jesus Loves Me!

Jesus said, "Let the little children come to me." —MATTHEW 19:14

Isn't it good to know Jesus loves you! He loves all children. Do you know how we know? There's a hint in this song. Let's sing it together.

JESUS LOVES ME!

Jesus loves me! This I know,
For the Bible tells me so.
Little ones to Him belong;
They are weak, but He is strong.

Jesus loves me! This I know,
As He loved so long ago,
Taking children on His knee,
Saying, "Let them come to Me."

Yes, Jesus loves me!
Yes, Jesus loves me!
Yes, Jesus loves me!
The Bible tells me so.

145

Bible Story

Matthew 19:13–15; Mark 10:13–16; Luke 18:15–17

So many people wanted to see Jesus that they were squishing Him. There were sick people and sad people and well people and happy people, and there were people who brought their children to meet Jesus.

"No children," Jesus' helpers said to the people. "Jesus doesn't have time for them."

Jesus heard what His helpers said. He stopped them right there. "Let the little children come to Me," Jesus said, and He began to bless the children.

Children are important to God. Children are important to Jesus. He loves them. He loves you!

Our Together Time

Let's Talk about It!

★ Why did Jesus' helpers want to send the children away?
★ What did Jesus say to His helpers?
★ How do you know Jesus loves you?

Share God's Love

Did you know that when you show kindness to others you share Jesus' love? There are lots of ways you can show kindness to others. You show kindness when you

✤ help someone,
✤ listen to someone,
✤ invite someone to play with you.

Draw a picture of one way you can show Jesus' love to others.

Prayer

Dear Jesus, thank You for loving me so much. I love You too. Amen.

God's Surprises

Come and see what the Lord has done. He has done
amazing things on the earth. —PSALM 46:8

What are some of your favorite surprises? A new toy? A trip to the zoo?
One of the most exciting things about God is that we never know what
wonderful thing He's going to do next. It's His surprise to us. Now let's
read together how God surprised Sammy. Then check out the Bible story
to see how God surprised the apostle Peter.

Sammy was sad. Grandpa had been sick
for a long time now. Sammy missed
Grandpa's visits and the walks they
used to take—just the two of
them. The shelf in Sammy's
room was filled with treasures
he and Grandpa had found—
feathers, shells, unusual rocks,
and a stick that looked like an
S for "Sammy." Grandpa
called them God's surprises.

Just then Sammy heard
three knocks, then the
doorbell. It was Grandpa's
special knock. Sammy
dashed to the front door.
"Grandpa, you're the best
one of God's surprises ever!"

149

Matthew 17:24–27

When Jesus lived on earth, He paid taxes, just as people do today. One day His friend Peter came to tell Jesus they didn't have any money to pay their taxes. That didn't bother Jesus at all.

"Go fishing, Peter. You will catch a fish, and there will be a coin in its mouth. Use that to pay our taxes."

Peter had been fishing all his life, and surely he had *never* once found a coin in a fish's mouth. But he trusted Jesus. Soon Peter caught a fish, and it had a coin in its mouth. Peter used the money to pay their taxes.

Our Together Time

Let's Talk about It!
★ What did Jesus and Peter need?
★ What did Jesus tell Peter to do?
★ What big surprise did Peter get?

Share God's Love
Peter must have looked very surprised when he saw the coin in the fish's mouth. How do you look when you're surprised? Make your most surprised look in a mirror to see. Did it make you laugh?

> ### SURPRISE!
>
> For some more fun, have everyone in your family take turns looking surprised. Then have everyone look their most surprised when you say, "One, two, three, surprise!" while someone takes a picture. When you show the picture to others, tell them about God's surprises.

Prayer
Dear Jesus, thank You for sharing Your love with me and giving me what I need. I love You. Amen.

Jesus Heals

The Lord says, ". . . I will lead the blind along a way they never knew. . . . I will make the darkness become light for them." —ISAIAH 42:16

Being blind means you can't see anything. People who are blind learn special skills to help them do everyday tasks. Sometimes they have a guide dog that helps them or they might carry a long white stick with a red tip to help them know when to step up or down or go around something. The stick also helps others know the person is blind.

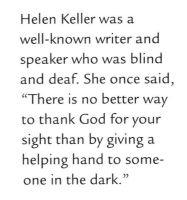

Helen Keller was a well-known writer and speaker who was blind and deaf. She once said, "There is no better way to thank God for your sight than by giving a helping hand to someone in the dark."

Bible Story

Mark 10:46–52

Jesus can do anything! He can heal sick people, and He can make blind people able to see again.

One day a crowd of people was following Jesus. A blind man, who was sitting by the road, kept calling out, "Jesus, please help me!" He was so loud that some of the crowd told him to be quiet.

Jesus ignored the crowd. He asked the blind man, "What would you like Me to do for you?"

The blind man said, "I want to see."

Jesus said, "You are healed because you believe." Now the man could see.

Our Together Time

Let's Talk about It!
★ What did Jesus ask the blind man?
★ What did Jesus do for the blind man?

Share God's Love
Share with your family or friends the story of how Jesus helped the blind man. Then to better understand how difficult it can be to be blind, try this experiment.

WHAT IS IT?

You'll need a bag and a blindfold. With a grownup's help, someone chooses small everyday objects—such as a rock, pencils, erasers, soap, toys, clothing, books—and places them in a bag. (No one who will be blindfolded should know what objects are in the bag.) Next the blindfolded person reaches into the bag and takes out one object. He or she has one minute to tell what the object is. Then it's someone else's turn to be blindfolded.

Prayer
Dear Lord, please help those who cannot see. Amen.

Be a Happy Giver

God loves the person who gives happily. —2 CORINTHIANS 9:7

Did you know that God wants us to give back to Him some of what He has blessed us with? Now you may be saying, "I'm just a kid. I don't have much money." Guess what? Money isn't the only way to give back to God. There are all kinds of ways to give, and the important thing is to do it with a happy heart.

Josh's friend Aaron had outgrown his winter coat, and there was no money for a new coat. Josh had a great idea. He would wear his big brother's old coat and give his own coat to Aaron. Mom, Dad, Josh's brother, Aaron, and Jesus liked Josh's "happy-giver" plan!

Mark 12:41–44

Jesus watched as people put their money in an offering box at the Temple. The rich people were giving a lot of money.

But then, from the back of the crowd came a very poor woman. She dropped her two copper coins into the box.

When Jesus saw her, He said to His followers, "This woman gave more than the rich people with many coins. She gave all the money she had."

Our Together Time

Let's Talk about It!
★ Who gave a lot of money?
★ Who gave all she had?
★ What did Jesus say about her gift?

Share God's Love
God can do great things with the small things you give, whether it is giving a small coin or a few hours of your time. Giving your time to help others is called volunteering, and it's a good way to give back to God. Ask your parents what your family can do to help others in your community. Maybe you can get your church involved by starting a contest in your Sunday school class. Divide the class into two teams and see which team can collect the most canned food for hungry families in your community.

Prayer
Dear Lord, help me to give with a happy heart.
Thank You for blessing me in so many ways. Amen.

Mighty Jesus!

I asked the Lord for help, and he answered me.
He saved me from all that I feared. —PSALM 34:4

Did you know that clouds can tell us a lot about the weather? But even if we learn everything about clouds, we still cannot control clouds or the weather. Only God and Jesus can do that. Check out today's Bible story and see what a mighty thing Jesus did. The next time you are outside, see if you can find any of the clouds listed below:

1. *Cirrus* clouds are high, thin wispy clouds that look like a horse's tail. These clouds don't give us a clue about the weather.
2. *Cirrocumulus* clouds are rows of white clouds sailing across the sky. They mean tomorrow's weather will be good.
3. *Nimbostratus* clouds are dark gray rain clouds. These clouds mean: get out your umbrella.
4. *Cumulonimbus* are "thunderhead" clouds. They have a flat base and a tall middle. These usually mean rain, thunder, lightning, and hail.

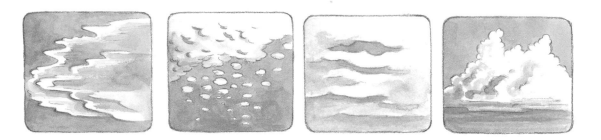

Mark 4:35–41

One day after Jesus had been teaching all day long, He and His friends got into a boat to go across the lake. Jesus was so tired He fell asleep. Before His friends could row across the lake, up came a strong storm. The wind began to whip around. Waves splashed high against the boat and began to fill it with water. It was a scary time.

Finally, Jesus' friends woke Him up. They were afraid. "Help us, or we'll drown!" they said. Jesus stood up and instead of grabbing an oar to help row, He spoke to the storm. "Quiet! Be still!" Jesus said. The wind stopped. The waves calmed down, and everyone was safe. Jesus is so mighty the wind and waves obey Him!

Our Together Time

Let's Talk about It!
★ What did Jesus do when He got into the boat?
★ What happened next?
★ What did Jesus say to the storm?

Share God's Love

Jesus is mighty. He made the storm stop as easy as turning on a light. If you were to crawl under a blanket, it would be dark and maybe a little scary. But if you were to turn on a flashlight under the blanket, it wouldn't be so scary. Try it and see. And the next time you and your family or friends are looking at the clouds, tell them how Jesus stopped a storm.

Prayer

Dear Lord, You are so mighty You can do anything. Thank You for being with me all the time—in stormy and sunny weather. Amen.

The Good Shepherd

"I am the good shepherd. The good shepherd gives his life for the sheep." —JOHN 10:11

Have you ever been to a zoo or farm where keepers care for sheep? In our together time today, we're going to see how a shepherd takes care of his sheep when they wander off. Jesus is called our Good Shepherd. Sometimes we are like sheep. We wander off. We get in trouble. We forget to follow Jesus who takes care of us as a shepherd takes care of his sheep. Psalm 23 in the Bible tells how the Lord is our Shepherd. Below is how it begins. Ask someone to help you find it and read the rest in your Bible.

The Lord is my shepherd.
I have everything I need.
He gives me rest in green pastures.
He leads me to calm water.
He gives me new strength.
—Psalm 23 (excerpt)

Bible Story

Luke 15:3–7

Jesus told a story about a shepherd who had 100 sheep. Every night when the shepherd brought his sheep home he counted them to make sure they were all there.

One night after he counted 99 sheep, there were no more sheep to count. One sheep was missing. The shepherd left his 99 sheep safe at home and went right out to find the one lost sheep. He looked high. He looked low. He looked everywhere. And finally he found the sheep.

The happy shepherd put the sheep on his shoulders—that's the way shepherds used to carry their sheep—and brought it home. The shepherd was so happy that he had a party with his friends to celebrate finding his lost sheep.

Our Together Time

Let's Talk about It!
- ★ Who is the Good Shepherd?
- ★ What did the shepherd do every night?
- ★ What did he do when he found one sheep missing?

Share God's Love

Doesn't it make you feel good to know that Jesus takes care of us just like the shepherd took care of his sheep! A fun game to help you remember that Jesus is our Good Shepherd, and that we need to follow Him in all that we do, is Follow the Shepherd.

> ### FOLLOW THE SHEPHERD
>
> Choose a shepherd, then stand in a line behind the shepherd. The shepherd says, "Follow me!" and then does an action like raise his or her hands or walk backward. Everyone must do exactly what the shepherd does. After the shepherd does three different things, he or she goes to the end of the line and the person in the front of the line is the shepherd. When everyone has had a turn, clap hands and start again.

Prayer

Dear Jesus, I'm so glad You care about me. Thank You for coming to search for me when I wander off in my heart and forget to follow You. Help me to love and obey You. Amen.

Forgiven

"Everyone who believes in Jesus will be forgiven.
God will forgive his sins through Jesus." —Acts 10:43

Have you done or said something you knew was not right? Jamie did . . .

Jamie knew it was against the rules to toss his football in the
house, but he did it anyway. Uh-oh, it hit the wall and . . .
CRASH! Jamie's mother came running into the room.

"Mom, I broke your lamp. I'm sorry. Can you
forgive me?" Jamie asked.

"Yes," she said. "But there will be consequences
for breaking the rules. I'll keep your football for two
days." Jamie helped clean up the mess. Then his
mother gave him a
big hug.

Here's some really great
news! No matter how
naughty we have been,
God will forgive us if we
ask Him.

Luke 15:11–24

There was a man who had two sons. The younger son decided he wanted the money that would be his when his father died while his father was alive. His father gave him the money. The son went off to another country and spent all his money on foolish things. After his money was gone, the son was hungry and alone. He got a job feeding pigs, and he was so hungry he even thought about eating the pigs' food.

Then he realized that his father's servants had more food than he had. He decided to go home, tell his father he was sorry, and ask if he could just be a servant. And that's what he did. To his surprise, when he went home, his father gave him a big hug and forgave him for all he had done.

Our Together Time

Let's Talk about It!
★ What did the younger son ask from his father?
★ What happened to the younger son's money?
★ When the younger son came home, what did his father do?

Share God's Love
Yuck! Can you imagine being so hungry that you would consider eating pig food? But isn't it comforting to know that if we mess up like the son in the Bible story, we can ask God, our heavenly Father, to forgive us and He will? He's like the father in the Bible story. He accepts us as we are when we ask for forgiveness.

Have you done something wrong? Talk to God right now and tell Him you are sorry. Ask Him to forgive you. And remember God wants you to forgive others just like He forgives you.

Prayer
Dear Lord, I ask You to forgive me for the wrongs I have done. Help me to do what is right. Amen.

When Jesus Cried

Jesus cried. —JOHN 11:35

Have you ever been sad when someone you loved died? Well, Jesus knows how sad it makes us feel when those we love die. He knows because He felt the same way when His friend Lazarus died. The Bible tells us that when Lazarus died, Jesus was so sad He cried. It's okay to be sad, and even to cry, but here's a happy thought to remember: some day we'll see our loved ones again in heaven. Till then we can remember the good times we had with them. And when those happy memories make us smile, that's okay too.

Tear drops fall like the rain
When our hearts are sad.
Jesus sees each tear that falls.
He makes sad hearts glad.
—Gwen Ellis

John 11:1–44

Jesus loved His friends Martha, Mary, and Lazarus.
One day when Jesus was away, Lazarus became ill.
When Jesus heard His friend was ill, Jesus waited
two days to start His trip to see His friends.
By the time Jesus arrived, Lazarus had been
dead for four days. Lazarus' sister Mary said,
"Jesus, if You had been here, my brother
would not have died." Jesus was so sad,
He cried. Then Jesus walked to Lazarus'
tomb and asked the people there to
move the stone from the entrance.

In a loud voice Jesus said, "Lazarus, come out!" And out of the tomb walked Lazarus, all wrapped up in burial clothes! He was alive and well.

Our Together Time

Let's Talk about It!
* Who became ill?
* What did Jesus do when He heard His friend Lazarus had died?
* What happened next?

Share God's Love
Were you surprised to learn that Jesus cried? What makes you sad? When friends are happy, it's easy to share their joy. But when friends are sad, it's hard to share their sorrow. Did you know you can help your friends through sad times by doing some very simple things to let them know you care:

❖ Take them cookies you helped bake.
❖ Listen to them.
❖ Be kind to them.
❖ Sit quietly next to them.
❖ Pray with them and for them.

And if you are the one who is sad—tell a grownup, talk to Jesus, and allow your friends to comfort you.

Prayer
Dear Lord, I know it's okay to be sad sometimes. Thank You for the happy memories I have of those who have gone to heaven to be with You. Amen.

A Thankful Heart

Thank the Lord because he is good. His love continues forever.
—PSALM 107:1

Has anyone ever thanked you for something you gave or did for him or her? How did it make you feel? The good thing about the words "thank you" is that they make both the one saying them and the one they're said to feel good. God wants you to have a thankful heart like the man in the Bible story we are going to read on the next page. Right now, practice having a thankful heart by playing the Thank-You Game.

THE THANK-YOU GAME

Put a lot of squares of different colored paper in a bag. Then pull out a piece and give thanks for something that color. For example: If the paper is white, what you might be thankful for is milk or snow. Green might be for grass or a favorite shirt.

177

Bible Story

Luke 17:11–19

One day Jesus was walking along a road when He saw ten men. They did not come close to Jesus because they had a skin disease called leprosy. The men called out to Jesus, "Please help us." Jesus healed all ten men. As they went on their way, the sores and bumps on their skin went away—which meant that their skin disease disappeared. They were well.

When one of the ten men saw that his skin was healed, he turned around and hurried back to thank Jesus for healing him. But he was the only one to say, "Thank you." He had a thankful heart.

Our Together Time

Let's Talk about It!
★ What was wrong with the ten men in the story?
★ What did they ask Jesus to do?
★ How many men said thank you?

Share God's Love
When you thank others for what they do for you, then you have a thankful heart. To share God's love with your family, here's a fun thing to do.

> As fast as you can, say all the things you're thankful for about each member of your family.

You may also want to make a list of these to use when you say your prayers. When you say your prayers, name each person and say what you are thankful for about that person.

Prayer
Dear Lord, thank You for my family. Here are some things I'm thankful for about each person in my family . . . Amen.

Let Me Serve You

When we have the opportunity to help anyone,
we should do it. —GALATIANS 6:10

"May I help you?" Where have you heard these words? From a server in a restaurant or a clerk in a store? But did you know that Jesus wants us all to find ways to serve one another? Not because it's a job, but because we have kind and loving hearts and think of others.

Here's a fun way to practice serving others. Offer to be the server at dinner. As the server, you should tell those being served what foods are available. After each person chooses what he or she would like to eat, write down their order and go get the food for them.

John 13:1–17

During Jesus' last days on earth, He and His closest followers had an evening meal together. It was the time of the Jewish Passover Feast. During their meal, Jesus got up from the table, took off His coat, wrapped a towel around His waist, and poured water into a big bowl.

Then He went from one of His friends to the next washing their dusty, maybe even smelly, feet.

He did this to show them how to serve one another. If Jesus, their leader, could act as their servant and wash their feet, they could do things to help and serve others too.

Our Together Time

Let's Talk about It!
★ What were Jesus and His followers doing?
★ During dinner, what did Jesus do?

Share God's Love
What are some ways you can serve others at home, at church, and at school? Following are some ideas, but there's a trick. Can you find the one idea that is *not* a way to serve others?

1. Rake the leaves in your grandma's yard.
2. Eat a piece of chocolate cake.
3. Give the clothes you've outgrown to someone who needs them.
4. Offer to help feed your neighbor's dog while they're on vacation.

(Did you guess number two is not a way to serve others? If so, you're right, and well on your way to serving others.)

Prayer
Dear Lord, if You can be a servant to others, so can I.
Help me find ways to serve others. Amen.

Happy Easter!

"God raised Jesus from death." —ACTS 13:34

Beautiful Easter eggs and cute bunny rabbits! Is that what you think about first when you think of Easter? Guess what . . . the celebration of Easter is about something much more important. It's the day many Christians celebrate Jesus rising from death. That's right! Jesus came back to life to show that He is our Savior, and if we believe in Him, when we die we'll live with Him in heaven.

He arose! He arose!
Hallelujah! Christ arose!
—Robert Lowry (1874)
   Excerpt from "Up from the Grave He Arose"

Matthew 27–28:10

After Jesus died on the Cross, His friends were very sad. They placed His body inside a tomb. Then they rolled a large heavy stone over it. Roman soldiers came, sealed the stone opening, and stood guard at the tomb.

On the third day after Jesus had died, some women went to His tomb. When they got there, they couldn't believe their eyes. The stone had been rolled away, and an angel of God was sitting on top of it. The tomb was empty. The angel said, "Don't be afraid. Jesus is alive. Tell His followers they'll see Him in Galilee." The women hurried to tell the others the good news—Jesus is alive!

Our Together Time

Let's Talk about It!
★ What happened to Jesus on the Cross?
★ Where did the women go?
★ What did the angel say?

Share God's Love
Aren't you glad Jesus rose from death to be our Savior so we can live with Him in heaven some day! Here's a fun way to celebrate Jesus coming back to life—even if it is not near Easter when you read this. Ask a grownup to boil some eggs and help you dye them. Before dipping the eggs in the dye, write on each one in crayon the name of the person you want to have the egg. When the eggs are dry, give each person the egg with his or her name on it, then say, "Hallelujah, Jesus is alive!"

> ### EASTER EGG DYE
>
> To make an Easter egg dye, put about $1/4$ teaspoon food coloring in $3/4$ cup of hot water. Then add 1 tablespoon of white vinegar to the water and stir.

Prayer
Dear Lord, I am so glad You are alive. Thank You for making it possible for me to go to heaven. Amen.

Good News!

"How beautiful is the person who comes to bring good news."
—ROMANS 10:15

What kind of news did you hear today? Was it good news? Was it not-so-good news? For fun, tell which of the following news flashes is good (G) and which is bad (B). See the answers below.

> **NEWS FLASHES**
>
> 1. A storm blew the roof off our house.
> 2. Today we built a snowman.
> 3. Our dog has four new puppies.
> 4. Jodi has a sore throat.

[1. B / 2. G / 3. G / 4. B]

Now here's the very best news the world ever heard: Jesus is God's Son, and He died to save us from sin. When we tell others about Jesus, we are sharing the Good News.

Acts 8:26–40

Philip was one of Jesus' followers who liked to tell people the Good News about Jesus. One day an angel spoke to Philip and told him to go to the desert road. On the road an important man from Ethiopia rode by in his chariot, reading the book of Isaiah. Philip ran alongside the chariot and asked if the man understood what he was reading.

The man said no, and asked Philip to explain it to him. Philip told him the Good News about Jesus. The man from Ethiopia believed what Philip told him and asked Philip to baptize him. After baptizing the man, Philip went to tell others the Good News.

Our Together Time

Let's Talk about It!
★ What did Philip tell the man from Ethiopia?
★ What did the man from Ethiopia ask Philip?

Share God's Love
Philip shared the Good News about Jesus, and you can too. Here's a fun way to practice.

> ### TELLING THE GOOD NEWS
>
> With a microphone, pretend to be a TV newsperson and in your own words tell the Good News about Jesus to your family and friends. Be sure and tell the whole story of how Jesus was sent by God to save us from our sins, and how Jesus died on the Cross, was buried, and came to life again so that we could have a home in heaven when we die.

Prayer
Dear Lord, I want to share Your Good News with everyone! Amen.

A Life That Shines

Christ himself died for you. And that one death
paid for your sins. —1 PETER 3:18

Have you ever told anyone about Jesus? How He's God's Son who died
to save us from our sin? Jesus wants us to tell others that He loves them
and will save them too. We can also show others how Jesus loves them
just by the way we act. When we live a life that's pleasing to God by
treating others with kindness, we're like a light shining in the darkness
to show them the way to Jesus.

A CHILD'S PRAYER

God make my life a little light,
Within the world to glow;
A tiny flame that burns so bright
Wherever I may go.
—M. Betham-Edwards

Bible Story

Acts 16:12–15

After Paul became a follower of Jesus, he went everywhere telling people the Good News about Jesus: How Jesus was God's Son, and how He died on the Cross for our sins.

One day Paul met a woman named Lydia. Her job was selling purple cloth. She loved God, but she didn't know about Jesus.

When Paul told Lydia who Jesus was and what He had done for her, she believed what Paul said and was baptized. All the people in her house believed and were baptized too.

Our Together Time

Let's Talk about It!
★ Why did Jesus die on the Cross?
★ How can we help others know this Good News?

Share God's Love
The news about Jesus saving us from our sin is too good to keep to ourselves. For a fun way to share the news, make a picture book to show your friends and family when you tell them about Jesus.

> **Page 1:** Draw a person with a sad face and a dark, dirty heart. This page stands for a person's heart before Jesus comes into it. They are dark with sin.
> **Page 2:** Draw a red cross. The red cross is for Jesus dying for our sins.
> **Page 3:** Draw a person with a clean heart. When we receive Jesus into our hearts, He takes away all the darkness and gives us a heart that is clean and new.
> **Page 4:** Draw a picture of a house using a yellow-gold crayon. The house stands for the mansion in heaven Jesus is making for all who believe in Him.

Prayer
Dear Lord, I believe You are God's Son. Thank You for dying for me so that I can someday live in heaven with You and God. Amen.

When It's Not Funny to Laugh

Do not let my enemies laugh at me. —PSALM 35:19

Sometimes when people laugh, it's not so good. Has anyone ever laughed at you when you weren't trying to be funny? If so, how did it make you feel? Not good, right? Did you know that God understands how we feel when we are laughed at or called names? It makes Him sad. Even the apostle Paul was laughed at because people didn't believe what he was saying about Jesus. In today's Bible story, find out why people laughed at Paul.

I laughed when my sister
fell down the stair.
I called her a clumsy teddy bear.

When baby brother
wrecked his sled,
I laughed and laughed 'til I turned red.

Then one day,
I slipped in the mud.
I went down with a great big
*   THUD!*

My friends wiggled and giggled
*   and pointed, you see.*
It wasn't any fun when they
*   laughed at me.*
—June Ford

Acts 17:16–34

The apostle Paul was a preacher who traveled all over telling people the Good News about Jesus. One day he was in the capital city of Greece—Athens. There was a place in Athens called Mars Hill. Men went there to talk to each other and to argue about everything. Paul saw an altar they had built. Written on it were the words "To the God who is not known."

Well, Paul began to tell them about our God and how He raised Jesus from death. Paul told them that they could know God too. Some of the people began to laugh at Paul. They were not ready to believe in God, and Paul could not change their minds.

Our Together Time

Let's Talk about It!
★ Who was Paul?
★ What did Paul tell the people about the "God who is not known"?
★ Why did some of the people laugh at Paul?

Share God's Love
Have you ever been like the people who laughed at Paul, laughing because you didn't believe someone? How would you feel if you found out what the person was saying was true? How would you feel if you were Paul and being laughed at? Tell a story about when laughter is not a good thing, like when someone laughs in a mean way. Now tell a story about when laughter is a happy thing.

Prayer
Dear Lord, You know that bullies do mean things.
Help them learn to be kind. Amen.

A Sudden Storm

All you who put your hope in the Lord be strong and brave.
—PSALM 31:24

When we have hope, we believe things will turn out for the best. God gives us hope because He is always doing what is best for us, and wanting us to do our best. And we have hope because we trust in God.

Twins Chester and Charlotte stood inside the school lobby watching as a cold wind whirled snowflakes outside. A sudden snowstorm had caught them unprepared for the walk home.

"We'd better go before the weather gets worse," Chester said.

"I still hope he'll come," Charlotte said. "I just know he will."

Just then the door swung open, and there stood the twins' dad holding their warm winter coats, hats, gloves, and boots. "Anyone need a ride home?"

201

Acts 27

Paul, the apostle, got on a big ship headed for Rome, Italy. After a time at sea, a strong wind came up and blew hard against the sails of the ship. The storm was so bad that the people on the ship lost all hope of staying alive. They thought they would die. But God sent an angel to tell Paul that all who sailed with him would be saved, but the ship would crash and be lost. Paul told them what God had said. He knew God would keep His promise. That gave everyone on the ship a great deal of hope. They weren't so frightened. When morning came, the ship hit a sandbank near an island and broke apart. Everyone who couldn't swim grabbed something that would float, like a piece of wood, and made it to the island's shore. They were all saved.

Our Together Time

Let's Talk about It!
★ Where was the apostle Paul going on the ship?
★ What happened on the way?

Share God's Love
Isn't God awesome! There were 276 people on-board the ship Paul was on and all of them survived the shipwreck. If you had been on that ship with Paul, how would you have felt when he told them they would not die?

FOR FUN, ACT OUT THE STORY

Use something like a blanket, sheet, string, or garden hose to make the shape of a boat. Put things such as pillows, boxes, and baskets in the boat. Choose something like an outside wall or the back of a sofa to be the island's shore. Choose one person to be Paul. The rest of the family can be the sailors and other passengers on the ship. Get inside the boat, and as someone reads the Bible story, act it out.

Prayer
Dear Lord, please help me to always have hope and to know that You are stronger than anything that can happen in my life. Amen.

A Home in Heaven

"No one has ever imagined what God has prepared for those who love him." —1 CORINTHIANS 2:9

Jesus made many promises, but the best is yet to come. He said He would have a special place ready for us when our lives on earth are over. That place is called heaven, and it's more beautiful than anything we've ever seen. It's so beautiful that if you were to draw a picture of what you think heaven might look like, you'd probably need to use all the colors in your crayon box. Think of an entire city made of gold and every kind of precious jewels, like green emeralds and blue sapphires and purple amethysts. Think of streets made of gold and gates made of pearl.

Well, heaven is like that. And it's a place without pain or sadness or death. And best of all, Jesus will be there. We will be with Him forever.

205

John 14:1–2; Revelation 21

One day Jesus talked with His friends and followers about heaven. He said, "Don't let your hearts be troubled. Trust in God. And trust in Me. There are many rooms in My Father's house. I would not tell you this if it were not true. I am going there to prepare a place for you."

God promises that in heaven no one will ever be sad again. No one will ever be sick again. Everything will be more wonderful than we have ever imagined. And we will be happy there forever.

207

Our Together Time

Let's Talk about It!

★ What did Jesus say He was going to do for us in heaven?
★ Will we be sad in heaven?
★ What's the best part of heaven?

Share God's Love

Wow! How wonderful it is to have heaven to look forward to! Here are some things that will help you think about how wonderful heaven will be:

1. Tell about the most beautiful place you have ever seen. (Heaven will be a thousand times more beautiful.)
2. Make up your own song about how wonderful heaven will be.

Prayer

Dear Lord, thank You for Your promise of heaven. I know You have lots of things for me to do first in this life. But it's so good to know You have a place waiting for me. Amen.

Index

Scriptures

God's Promises

ACTIVITIES

Crafts